The Marketers'

Customer Data Platform

Resource Book

First published 2019 by Berry Thompson, 5 Godalming Business Center, Woolsack Way, Godalming, Surrey GU7 1XW

Enquiries should be emailed **to** <u>info@berry-thompson.com</u>

We would like to acknowledge the support of the Customer Data Platform Institute.

ISBN 978-0-244-76071-7

Contents

1 What is a CDP and what problems does it solve? [1]

Why Customer Data Is Important?

Today's customers simply assume that your company knows – and remembers – who they are, what they've done, and what they want, at all times and across all channels. Marketers and marketing technologists know that gathering and acting on unified customer information isn't easy. In fact, just a few companies have actually achieved complete integration. The rest are battling with technology, strategy, budgets, organizations, staff skills, and other obstacles to success.

But customers don't know or care about those challenges. If you don't meet their expectations, they'll assume you don't care about them and take their business to somebody else they believe will treat them better. Whether those other firms will really give them a better experience almost doesn't matter: once you've lost them, you'll have to fight twice as hard to get them back.

---

[1] This introduction to customer data platforms has been sourced from the Customer Data Platform Institute

No wonder so many marketers have made a unified customer experience their highest priority.

Why Customer Data Platforms?

A unified customer experience is impossible without unified customer data. Most data originate in separate systems that weren't designed to share it with anything else. Traditional methods for collecting that data into unified customer profiles, such as an enterprise data warehouse, have failed to solve the problem. Newer approaches, like "data lakes", have collected the data but failed to organize it effectively.

The Customer Data Platform is an alternative approach that has had great success at pioneering companies. A CDP puts marketing in direct control of the data unification project, helping to ensure it is focused directly on marketing requirements. CDPs apply specialized technologies and pre-built processes that are tailored precisely to meet marketing data needs. This allows a faster, more efficient solution than general purpose technologies that try to solve many problems at once.

Customer Data Platform Definition

"A Customer Data Platform is packaged software that creates a persistent, unified customer database that is accessible to other systems".

This definition has three critical elements:

- "packaged software": the CDP is a prebuilt system that is configured to meet the needs of each client. Some technical resources will be required to set up and maintain the CDP, but it does not require the level of technical skill of a typical data warehouse project. This reduces the time, cost, and risk and gives business users more control over the system, even though they may still need some technical assistance.

- "creates a persistent, unified customer database": the CDP creates a comprehensive view of each customer by capturing data from multiple systems, linking information related to the same customer, and storing the information to track behaviour over time. The CDP contains personal identifiers used to target marketing messages and track individual-level marketing results.- "accessible to other systems": data stored in the CDP can be used by other systems for analysis and to manage customer interactions.

2 What's under the bonnet of a CDP?

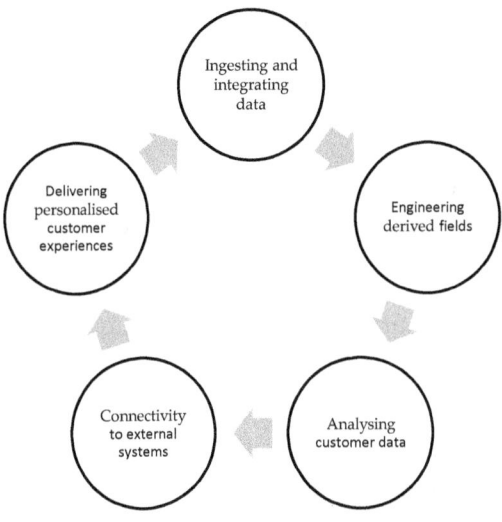

Ingesting and integrating data

CDPs ingest customer data from multiple sources.
Typically, these will include websites, transactional,
retail and email systems. All data received by a CDP
will relate in some shape or form to a customer.

The data is usually sent to a CDP using an API or via an
SFTP site.

As new data is ingested, each record goes through what
is called the 'purning' process; this is the stage at which
the record's personal identifier(s) are matched against

all other customer records that are held in the CDP until a match is or is not found. At this point the data may be matched into an existing single customer view or a new one created. Each recognised customer is given a permanent unique record number or 'purn'.

The single customer view is at the heart of a CDP and is central to all the rest of its functionality. A good CDPs' functionality is rooted in the knowledge that people have multiple identifiers, and that these identifiers can all change over time.

By an identifier we mean any data element that is uniquely associated with an individual; these can include a mobile phone number, email, cookie ID, postal address, customer reference or landline number.

Over time many or all of these are likely to change for an individual, but the CDP should keep a history for each individual of every version of these, although regarding the latest versions as most likely to be current. This collection of identifiers is what it calls on to build the single customer view.

The data in a CDP is held in what is called a schema. This is the way in which the data is organised. Every organisation using a CDP will need their own schema although within an industry, schemas will have a lot of similarities.

Engineering derived data

Engineered data is important for the value it provides for selecting specific customer groups for communications, or developing customer insight. It can comprise any variable that can be calculated using an algorithm or other means from the raw data in the customer data platform.

Data engineering can take many forms, from simple examples like banding variables such as age, to more complex ones like keeping a counter on customer's total historic value. A major use of engineered data is in developing and recording scores derived from algorithms such as propensity models.

An example of an engineered data field is where we want to know what each customer has contributed to a business after the cost of recruiting them. Here we can use historic purchase data for each individual in say their first and second year since recruitment, deduct the cost of recruitment which can be derived the channel they came in from, and the cost of communications sent to them in the same period which is held in the contact history area, and calculate an individual customer contribution.

Engineered data is updated at an individual level every time a relevant event happens; so, each new ticket sold or home shopping purchase can lead to a changed score in the engineered data section.

A great benefit of engineered data is that it allows you to base axis for charts or selections for campaigns on these additional variables.

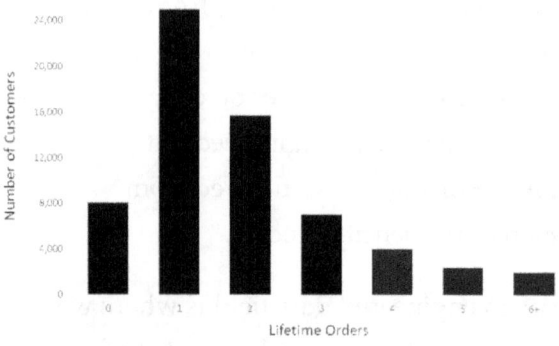

Figure 1 - example chart using engineered data

This allows for campaigns based on behavioural triggers (e.g. customers whose purchases have declined this quarter compared to last quarter) as well as on static customer data.

Analysing customer data

A CDP is essential for gaining a full and accurate understanding of customer behaviour. For instance, without a CDP that combines web browsing history with transactions, it would not be possible to understand the relationship between the two.

Again, if individual contact history is not held against a customer record then the effectiveness of campaigns that are sent to the customer, and to which the customer may respond through different channels, cannot be properly measured.

The CDP builds the single customer view and it is against this that customer analysis can take place. It provides the dataset that becomes the one authoritative source of information about customer behaviour for an organisation. With this in place decision makers have a firm basis on which to proceed.

There are so many aspects to the analytical tools that can be used to analyse customer data that there is little merit in trying to list them all. Some are built into the CDP and others require data to be first extracted from the CDP and then transferred to them. What matters is that they have the best possible customer data set to analyse.

So, the results from customer analysis form the basis on which key decisions about customer marketing can be made. These include such areas as customer recruitment (targeting and channel choice), digital planning, product development, customer relationship management, salesforce management, pricing, and even corporate mergers and company valuations.

Given how important these decisions are, it makes good sense when designing a CDP to first start with a list of the kind of results that will be required from customer analysis so that for instance data is held with sufficient granularity to make these possible.

Connectivity to external systems

The CDP can support other systems in their personalisation and management of customer communications.

Typical examples are providing customer selections for email marketing systems, customer segmentations for web personalisation technology, names and addresses for postal marketing, and target audiences for social media. So just as the CDP ingests data from multiple sources it also provides selected data to external systems.

These connections are usually made via an API or via transfer of data to an SFTP site.

Delivering personalised customer experiences

Within the CDP we expect to find functionality for the
selection of specific customer groups either on a one-off
or on a recurring basis. These groups are usually
selected for output to external systems that manage the
actual communications.

The selections themselves can be simple, and based on
Boolean logic rules, or they may be more complex, and
based on propensity scores applied within the
engineered data. They can also be based on triggers,
such as a new customer having just been recruited.

The CDP needs to enable these different types of
selection, and crucially record what contacts each
individual customer has been selected for. Functionality
is also required for test and control, and for including
source codes with the selection.

Associated with delivering personalised customer
experiences needs to be functionality for measuring the
results of campaigns. This is often automated within the
design of the CDP, and should always include the
ability to attribute results such as orders back to
campaigns, even if they respond through different
channels.

3 How do you measure the payback from a CDP?

By its nature a CDP changes the way that a company interacts with its customers at every stage from recruitment to reactivation. It will help an organisation use recruitment channels in such a way that higher value clients are recruited, it will help provide personalised and relevant communications at each stage in the customer journey, and it will help target those dormant customers that can be re-activated.

The consequence of this is that there is no single metric by which the value of a CDP can be measured, but instead a series of metrics that are derived from multiple changes to the status quo. The good news is that these can all be included in spreadsheet and added up.

We would like to introduce you to two case studies from a retail environment as examples of how a business case for a CDP was developed.

Both of the companies maintained detailed reports of the costs and results from all of their current direct communications activities. These formed the basis from which many of the benefits from introducing a CDP could be estimated.

In each case workshops were held to examine where a CDP could add value, and lists of benefit streams were developed. In addition, areas where time savings would result from automation were identified.

Managers were then asked to estimate the anticipated level of improvement they would expect when a CDP was introduced, in percentage terms, and a very conservative view taken of the expected uplifts.

There remained a lengthy list of important but largely unquantifiable benefits such as improved customer experience or improved business continuity when staff left.

- *So where did the benefits come from?*

We divided these into improvements to marketing operations, and to planning activities:

Category	Area impacted	UniFida impact
Operations	Direct mail and email campaigns	- Integration of outbound communications across all channels, particularly email and mail - Welcome packs and welcome emails based on initial purchase

		and known pre-existing customer characteristics such as browsing history - Early inclusion of new customers in campaigns - Next best action taking account of purchase propensities, browser interests and email opens - Managing customer contact density based on individual customer propensity to purchase - Ease of introducing tests and evaluating results - Where a company owns several brands, the CDP opens up cross-sale opportunities
	Web, email and catalogue personalisation	- Personalisation (via Fresh Relevance or selected provider) incorporating

		underlying customer characteristics such as customer value, customer attrition risk, and customer sale responsiveness in combination with recent on-line activity into the personalised experience - Catalogues can be personalised by product preferences - Maintaining history of personalised offers on the customer record
	Implementation of data science	- Engineered data derived from data science algorithms like segmentations or propensity scores used in all areas of customer selections and analysis - All engineered data fields updated every time new customer data arrives

	GDPR	- Customer search, and automated fulfilment of SARs and the right to be forgotten - Maintenance of preference records
	Customer feedback	- Can include customer survey capability e.g. for post purchase feedback - Feedback can be based on emojis
	Cold list processing	- Hierarchical merge-purge of cold lists - Response reporting integrated with house-file and results from above the line channels
	Identity resolution	- Individual deduplication based on multiple personal identifiers - Automated access to external PAF and suppression suppliers

Category	Area impacted	UniFida impact
		either at point of data entry or exit
Category	Area impacted	UniFida impact
Planning	Overall marketing planning	- Personalised dashboards for all users who can build or select their own charts using both on-line and off-line data - Real time user structured reports on sales and campaign responses leading to swift changes in campaign planning - Longer term reports on customer value and retention - Marketing analytics based on a sound CDP - Democratising of decision making from shared customer knowledge

		- Customer data visualisation in Tableau including geographical representation
	Speed to implement step changes	- Acceleration of project delivery with marketeers in control of their data and their technology
	Recruitment budget allocation	- Ongoing reports of customer LTV by recruitment channel (historic or predicted) - Enabling selection of channels and media based on customer longer term value delivered
	Business continuity	- The logic behind campaign selections and reports as well as results history kept secure

		- Ease of reuse for future campaign activity by all staff members
Savings	Time savings from accelerated operational activities	- Ease of making campaign selections and developing reports - Simplicity of organising customer data outputs - Reduction in the workload for IT

What were the results of the business casing exercises?

The following table shows in indexed and % fashion the end results. The calculations were all done on per annum basis as the cost of the CDP was to be charged in that way.

	Client A	Client B
Current net contribution from Direct Marketing activities (index)	100	54

Uplift in net contribution from introducing a CDP	17%	16.5%
Cost of the CDP as a % of net contribution	2%	4%
ROI from the CDP	8.2	4.2

The current net contribution was the calculation of the value obtained from marketing communications after deducting their costs. The ROI was calculated as the ratio of the uplift in net contribution over the cost of the CDP.

In both cases it made much more sense to invest in introducing the CDP than in increasing the current level of marketing communications spend.

- *Our conclusions*

A decision to invest in a CDP will usually involve looking carefully at the many aspects of the business that are going to be impacted by it. It is only by assembling these multiple benefit streams that a full business case can be built. However, if your results are like these, the case for making the investment can be extremely strong.

4 Who should have a CDP and who should not?

CDPs are suitable for any organisation that has:

- A significant number of customers (say 10,000 +)
- A direct relationship with those customers
- Customer data in several places on-line and off-line
- An appetite to use its customer data to increase customer value
- A marketing team that could use and get benefit from a CDP

When we talk to an organisation about the possibility of introducing a CDP, we like to probe several areas to find out more about their readiness, and the extent to which one is needed. This is the checklist we use:

Concerning organisational readiness

- Given that introducing one would cost money would you have internally the knowledge and resources to develop the business case?
- Is there a natural sponsor and /or project manager in your organisation for a customer data platform?

- Do you have an internal IT function and would they support the introduction of a customer data platform?
- Are marketers in your organisation frustrated by not having direct access to customer data for making campaign selections and undertaking customer analysis?
- Would it help if your organisation understood more about how customers are performing?

About how you currently manage your customer data
- Do you keep your customer data in many different places?
- Can you list all the places you would need to go to for a single view of your customers?
- Can you link customer browsing to their off-line data?
- Do you have problems deduplicating customers when running campaigns?
- Can you co-ordinate email and paper campaigns?
- Is customer data management dependant on a single individual?

About how to improve ROI from campaigns
- Can you easily attribute sales back to campaigns?
- How do you currently go about campaign reporting?
- Can you make campaign selections based on customer segments, scores or profiles?
- Is it easy to introduce split run tests and evaluate the results?
- Can you personalise your emails and browser experience?

Regarding GDPR
- Do you have a single central repository of customer consents?
- Are your consent records easily linked to your campaign selection processes?
- Do you have difficulty fulfilling subject access requests or the right to be forgotten?
- Do you automatically remove customer records that are too old to be of value?

About marketing planning
- Do you have access to dashboards giving you up to date information on customer performance?

- Do you understand the longer-term value of your customers and is this differentiated by different recruitment sources and customer types?
- Can you manage your choice of recruitment channels and media based on ROI?
- Is there a single place where all marketing decision makers can go to for customer information?

5 How a CDP makes marketing accountable?

Accountability in marketing becomes more and more important as channels multiply, and customers receiving messages through one channel may respond through another.

However, having a CDP in place makes what would otherwise be extremely difficult often much more straightforward.

The CDP will contain at a customer level:

- Every transaction
- All direct contacts like email or SMS

What it won't contain are indirect contacts such as outdoor advertising, TV, door-drops etc.

So how does the accountability process work?

1 Measuring existing customer value delivered over time

With all the transactions recorded for each customer, the value delivered by each customer becomes a calculation of the value of the customer transactions, minus the cost of providing the goods or service, minus the costs of any direct marketing the customers received such as catalogues. These calculations can take place in the CDP every time an event happens such as a new purchase or a fresh contact.

2 Measuring direct campaign value

Knowing who received the campaign, what it cost, and what the customers did afterwards during an outcome window you set, the CDP calculates the value generated by every direct campaign. With one caveat. You will need to set control groups whom you don't contact but which are in all other respects like the ones you do contact. This will allow you to deduct the natural proclivity of the customers to buy your product.

3 Measuring recruitment value by indirect channel

This is not always possible but the CDP will record recruitment channel source whenever it can.

In the case of customers arriving via social channels this can be tracked through your website. If they arrive from other channels such as media inserts or door-drops then you will need to rely on the customer providing a source code.

The good news is that for the cases where you do know the source you will also know their downstream longer-term customer value.

So for instance PPC advert recruits can be tracked over time and their subsequent customer value generated calculated.

4 Measuring recruitment value through channel and customer type

Age band	Sum assured	Channel 1	Channel 2	Channel 3	Channel 4
25-45	Low				
	Medium low				
	Medium				
	Medium high				
	High				
46-55	Low				
	Medium low				
	Medium				
	Medium high				
	High				
56-65	Low				
	Medium low				
	Medium				
	Medium high				
	High				
66+	Low				
	Medium low				
	Medium				
	Medium high				
	High				

Figure 2- this chart developed for a life assurance company shows the net contribution by the average customer in each group over 24 months (the actual numbers have been changed into grey colour bands where the highest contributors are light, lowest positive contributor dark)

Different channels attract different types of people. These different types will provide different levels of customer value.

In many cases you will collect some core data on your recruited customers, so that you can categorise them. That may be what they bought, or date of birth, or gender, or geodemographic information derived from their postcode. When combined with the source channel that can give you rich insights into where your recruitment marketing is profitable, and where it is not. You may find that older people recruited through channel X are very highly contributory whereas younger people recruited through the same channel are not.

6 Using a CDP for direct marketing campaigns

Direct marketing campaigns are central to a CDP's functionality, but the selection process does need some detailed logic behind it if it is to give you the controls you need.

We have put together a checklist of the campaign features that we regard as important when selecting a CDP, although different industries and environments may wish to add or subtract from this list.

Selections can be driven by engineered data

What we mean by engineered data are variables that can be used in a selection and that are derived from the raw data ingested by the CDP. Examples are customer value, propensity to purchase, or risk of attrition. These engineered data variables should be updated every time that data enters your CDP. In practice we find that they are much more likely to be used in selection logic than individual data values.

A choice of selecting individuals or households

This is fairly self-explanatory except that when selecting at a household level you have to decide whom in the household you want to target. It could be the person with the highest customer value, or the last one to place an order.

Having a choice of output templates

CDPs connect to many different customer contact channels from email service providers to SMS text messaging. Your CDP needs first to output the correct data for the channel in question, and then to be able to include added personalisation data for example referring to your most recent purchase.

Using selection criteria

Very frequently a selection driven by Boolean logic is at the heart of the selection process. You need to be able to choose from a list of available selection criteria, apply the =, >, < style logic, and then get a quick count of how many people have been selected as each criterion is added in. It is helpful if your CDP can show you the actual customer numbers behind each value in the variable you are thinking of using. You also need to be able to add groups together by 'or' statements such as 'men over 50' or 'women over 40'.

Sometimes you may want to view and select the numbers of customers available using two criteria at a time. For instance, you could want to see a table of available customers both by their response propensity score and by the type of merchandise they most often buy. You can then pick the customers in any of the cells in the table to build up your selection.

Controlling the selection numbers to output

Having made your selection you could find that you ended up with more customers than you wanted. In this case you need to be able to reduce the numbers down to for instance the volume you have print ready for. In this case you may wish to output customers from the selection using a criterion, such as descending customer value or ascending recency.

Allocating source codes to selected groups

You may wish to give all of your selection the same source code or you may wish to split it up so that you can measure the response levels from different types of customer. You may wish to split the selected group into randomly selected tests, and to allocate percentages of the selection to each test. And finally, you may wish to introduce controls that you don't contact but which are marked by their source code so that you can compare what they purchase without any stimuli being applied.

Viewing samples of those selected

One of the worst outcomes of a selection is that you believe that you have got everything right, only to find that in reality the selection you made picked some of the people you did not want to include. The best way to avoid this is to view a random sample of your selection before you release it.

Applying seed lists

A seed list is a short list of people, often colleagues working in your company, whom you want to receive all your campaigns when they go out. The seeds are then kept in the picture of what is going on. Your CDP should allow you to build seed lists, add or subtract people from them, and then add them to campaigns.

Loading to contact history

You will need to be able to decide whether you want the fact that someone has been selected for a campaign to be stored on their customer record. Normally you will, and the record will then show the source code of the campaign they received. In addition, you may wish to record the individual cost of that campaign so that you can include this in a customer contribution calculation.

Adding campaign metadata

For every campaign you select you will want to complete metadata describing that campaign. This will include a brief description of the campaign with the channel used and the programme type. You may also want to include financial data like the cost per 1000, or the cost of the goods being sold. To support attribution of subsequent orders to your campaign you may wish to set a time window during which that is legitimate. This campaign metadata is then used in the detailed reporting of campaign results.

Scheduling repeat selections

Campaigns may be one off or you may wish them to repeat; for instance, welcome packs may need to be sent out the day after a new customer joins up, or you may want to ask for customer feedback five days after an order has been delivered. These repeating or trigger campaigns should be set to happen automatically.

Generating custom audiences for social media

Social media like Facebook ask for custom audiences from you so that they can target lookalikes. It is important that the selection of current customers you make for custom audiences are selected from the type of customers you really do want to recruit, for instance high value customers with a low likelihood of attrition. Your CDP should support the selection of custom audiences.

Allowing you to save and copy a previous selection logic

In reality most of your campaigns will be repeats, but what you want to save are not the actual people selected but the logic that lay behind the campaign selection process.

7 Using a CDP for web-site and email personalisation

Website and email personalisation are now taken for granted when visiting a website or receiving communications from any major brand.

The technology that does this has even acquired a name; an 'Experience Optimisation Platform or EOP'.

The website or email personalisation can take many forms; pop-ups, recommendations, countdowns, dropped basket follow ups, dynamic content, and even social proof (e.g. the average customer satisfaction score was 4.5 stars for this product you are looking at).

However, an EOP needs more than just a recent history of what an individual has been browsing on a website to function properly.

A particular browsing customer may have been a high value customer in the past but has been dormant for over a year. Another customer may have a known history of only purchasing from sales offers, and a third may be a serial returner. Each of these will respond to very different offers.

The role of the CDP is to provide the EOP with knowledge like this so that they can serve the right offer at the right moment.

This is best done by giving customers segment scores from the CDP like 'valuable but dormant' or 'regular bargain hunter'.

The scores can then play their part in the decision process that decides what form of personalisation to make to a customer (although this clearly only applies to recognised customers, and not to unknown browsers).

The EOP technologists have even christened your CDP data as 'slow moving' to contrast it with your 'fast-moving-real-time browser activities'.

This process of linking a CDP to an EOP works because behind the scenes each 'experience' served to you on a website only happens because your behaviour has conformed to a set of rules that qualify you for it.

More often than not EOPs function without getting a feed of customer segments from a CDP, but when they do the experience and the results obtained from that are very much stronger.

8 How does a CDP identify individuals?

Identity resolution is at the heart of developing a successful CDP. The issue now is that we all have multiple ways of being identified and over time each of those ways may change.

For instance, personally identifiable information or PII as it is frequently called can include:

Full name,
Home address
Email address

National Insurance number
Passport number
Driver's license number
Credit card numbers
Date of birth
Mobile telephone number
Landline telephone number
Log in details
Customer number held in a cookie
Internet Protocol (IP) address
Processor or device serial number
Unique device identifier

Some of these can uniquely identify an individual on their own, whilst others will require some additional item of data to be sure of pointing to an individual.

Every organisation using a CDP will have their own mix of PII data and so the rules for matching individuals together will need to be adjusted to what is available.

However, given that some of these identifiers will change, for instance you may use several different email addresses, the CDP needs to maintain a history of all the versions of a PII that can be attributed to an individual.

When new data reaches a CDP, one of the first tasks is to match the incoming PIIs to existing PIIs, and to match records where possible, or if that does not succeed, create a new permanent unique reference number (PURN) for the individual.

Occasionally new data can arrive that succeeds in linking two records together that had previously been kept separate. For example, two emails may have been kept apart until they are both found to be linked to the same mobile phone number.

When setting up a CDP for your organisation, identifying what data will be used as PIIs, and how they should be employed on their own or in combination with other PIIs to create a unique identity, is a key task.

9 What engineered data should you build into a CDP?

Every type of organisation will have their own requirements for engineered data, although there is considerable overlap between these.

The key reason for developing a set of engineered data fields to hold in your CDP is that it removes the need to recalculate them every time you want to use them.

They are used in a number of ways including customer analysis, building charts, making selections, and reporting on marketing performance.

They provide an important level of consistency. For instance, if age-bands are always defined in the same way for an organisation, much confusion can be avoided.

The engineered data fields are refreshed every time new data arrives. For instance, if you have an engineered data field for historic life time value, then each new order will augment this.

Here is a list of some of the more commonly used engineered data fields:

Age band
Consents for specific marketing activities
Customer segment
Frequency of purchases in previous period
Historic customer value
Predicted customer value after first order
Predicted customer value at recruitment
Preferred channel
Principle historic purchase category
Probability of reactivation
Recency since last purchase

Risk of attrition

Sensitivity to price reductions

10 How does a CDP interact with AI and Data Scientists, and vice versa?

There are many interlinked processes involving CDPs and data scientists and their AI tools.

Most frequently AI is applied to data that is outside the CDP itself when the machine learning itself is going on. This does not need to be the case, but at present most CDPs do not have built -in machine learning capabilities. We suspect that this will change as AI use becomes more widespread.

So normally the data scientist will be analysing customer data and developing segmentations or predictive models, with or without AI tools, in a separate environment to the CDP.

However, the CDP is normally the source of the data with which the data scientist works.

Furthermore, the CDP is the tool that then allows the resultant algorithms or rule sets to be applied to live data in the CDP, and generate actions such as inclusion or exclusion from specific marketing activities.

Take an example of wanting to understand how browsing on a web-site is linked to purchasing;

- The CDP ingest the browsing activity data
- The CDP records the purchase events
- The CDP exports the combined data and the data scientists uses external tools to search for correlations

Or another example of developing a model to predict which dormants might be re-activated:

- The CDP holds the records of the dormant customers and has recorded which ones have re-activated
- The CDP will hold other dormant customer descriptors such as purchase history before they went dormant
- The data scientist will use this combined data outside the CDP to build a dormancy re-activation model
- The resultant algorithm is applied within the CDP to select customers for reactivation campaigns

11 How does a CDP measure and utilise customer longer term value?

Customer longer term value (CLTV) is a key metric for several aspects of the marketing process, and often overlooked by people chasing cost of acquisition (COA) as their goal for setting recruitment targets.

CLTV can be used for:

- Measuring the effectiveness of recruitment channels. In this case provided the source of recruits can be successfully allocated, which for indirect media may be difficult, then their effectiveness can be understood and budget allocated accordingly. Different channels by their nature attract different types of customer, and these different customer types will arrive with different levels of affluence and proclivity to buy your product.
- Managing high value or VIP customers differently to low value. This is common sense but what is less well known is that it is often possible to predict who is going to turn out to be a high value customer from their first order with a reasonable degree of accuracy. This is an

example of a model based on first order to predict first year's value.

- Reactivating dormants. Put simply it's worth allocating more budget to dormants who had previously been high value customers than low value.

A CDP is the ideal tool for recording individual customer value as it records every transaction the customer makes, and the cost of communications sent to that customer. At this point engineered data fields are required to compartmentalise value into years from recruitment, and then deduct from that the cost of goods including the cost of providing them.

We would in fact recommend abandoning CLTV in favour of customer year one value, customer year two value etc. as lifetime value depends on when people are recruited and how long they have been customers.

This development of customer value on a cohort basis can then be used as a key planning tool when you are looking at the level of customer recruitment you need to hit your targets.

12 Setting up tests and controls in a CDP

Using tests and controls are at the heart of good marketing practice, and the CDP is a key tool in that process.

This happens first because the single customer view ensures deduplication of customers, and second because the CDP enables people selected for campaigns to be put into different groups, and their subsequent activities tracked.

So, the CDP capabilities required for running tests (by the way, we regard controls as just another form of test but one in which no communications are sent) are as follows:

-   Randomly segmenting selected customers into different groups for one or more tests, and being able to do that on a % split for each test
-   Labelling the groups with different source codes according to their test cell
-   Monitoring sales post test, including order attribution, so that the performance of the different tests can be compared with the control.

13 The role for a CDP in managing GDPR requirements

The General Data Protection Regulation makes an assumption that organisations involved with personal data have, supporting that, a perfect single customer view, where all of a data subject's information is held and collated. Without that it is difficult to fulfil subject access requests, exercise the right to be forgotten, or to know what consents have been provided by an individual.

In reality most organisations without a CDP, and most don't have one, find these things very difficult to do.

CDPs were not developed for GDPR, indeed most were starting to be developed before GDPR was even first thought of, but because of their innate capability to link and store all known data concerning an individual, they provide a very strong basis from which to deal with all GDPR questions.

What follows is a short checklist of what your CDP needs to be able to do to enable you to comply with GDPR:

- Build and maintain a single customer view for each person for whom you hold personal data, including both on-line and off-line information
- In the case of a subject access request, allow you to search for an individual, and request that all the information you hold about them is presented in a clearly understandable form. At this stage you may wish to email or post the information to the data subject.
- Store all consent information allowing or disallowing marketing activities and profiling. Each consent action is to be held separately and to contain the date/time it was made, the means by which it was obtained, the statement that the consent was about, the marketing activity it applies to, the channel it applies to, and whether it is an opt-in or opt-out.
- Link the consents stored to your communications activity so that opt-outs or opt-ins can be applied to selections (and where the consents provided conflict, determine which trumps which).

	Marketing	Profiling	Third Party
Email			
Facebook			
Mail			
SMS			
Telephone			

Figure 3 – GDPR matrix showing where consents can be applied

- Apply bulk legitimate interest flags to customers where applicable so that they can receive communications even if they have not consented.
- Exercise the right to be forgotten when requested so that all personal information relating to an individual is deleted, without deleting the non-personal data which can still be used for reporting purposes. However there need to be flags for situations when an individual should not be forgotten, for instance when they have an active contract or account.
- Inform upstream systems which feed your CDP that an individual has requested to be forgotten, with details of where their data came from, and when it was transferred to the CDP.

14 Using the CDP to record on-line customer engagement

Your CDP will be receiving browsing information from all recognisable people whose on-line activities have been ingested into your single customer view.

Clearly before they are recognisable you can start to store an individual's browsing activity but that will not be able to be matched into the single customer view until they provide some tangible evidence like an email address or a mobile number.

When setting up your CDP you will need to decide which browsing activities need to be recorded, how they are to be described, and whether you want to record any summary information that explains the extent to which they have been active on your website.

The browsing activity may be used to trigger email, SMS or mail campaigns and may be used as an indicator of likelihood to purchase.

15 Using the CDP to manage contact density

We strongly recommend that you use your CDP to record all customer contact events. These can be outbound like emails, or inbound such as calls to your call-centre, or landings on your website.

Having the contacts stored allows you to measure the effectiveness of your communications by subsequent purchases, whether or not a media code is provided.

It also allows you to set rules so that you can control the level of contact an individual receives; for instance, no more than three emails per week, or twelve catalogues in a season.

A more sophisticated user will want to look at the relationships between the number of contacts and the amount of purchases.

Our experience is that for customers with a high expected value of purchase that they will respond well to multiple communications, whereas for customers with low expected purchases, the return from sending high volumes of communications is little more than from sending low volumes.